SPARKNOTES

Power Tactics

FOR THE NEW SAT

THE NEW SAT
VOCABULARY BUILDER

SPARK NOTES

A DIVISION OF BARNES & NOBLE PUBLISHING

Spark Educational Publishing
A Division of Barnes & Noble Publishing
120 Fifth Avenue
New York, NY 10011

ISBN 1-4114-0282-0

Please submit changes or report errors to *www.sparknotes.com/errors*

Printed and bound in Canada.

Written by Doug Tarnopol

"Flocabulary" by Alexander Rappaport and Escher

CONTENTS

INTRODUCTION

Truly effective SAT preparation doesn't need to be painful or time-consuming. SparkNotes' *Power Tactics for the New SAT* is proof that powerful test preparation can be streamlined so that you study only what you need. Instead of toiling away through a 700-page book or an expensive six-week course, you can choose the *Power Tactics* book that gets you where you want to be a lot sooner.

Perhaps you're Kid Math, the fastest number-slinger this side of the Mississippi, but a bit of a bumbler when it comes to words. Or maybe you've got the verbal parts down but can't seem to manage algebraic functions. *Power Tactics for the New SAT* provides an extremely focused review of every component on the new SAT, so you can design your own program of study.

If you're not exactly sure where you fall short, log on to **testprep.sparknotes.com/powertactics** and take our free diagnostic SAT test. This test will pinpoint your weaknesses and reveal exactly where to focus.

Without a reasonable amount of SAT vocabulary under your belt, all the tricks and strategies in the world are not going to help you with the Critical Reading and Writing sections of the exam. You've made the right decision because in a few short hours, you will have learned several powerful methods for expanding your vocabulary, as well as how to gain points with that new knowledge. No sweat, no major investment of time or money, no problem.

So, let's not waste any time: go forth and conquer SAT vocabulary so you can get on with the *better parts* of your life!

ABOUT THE NEW SAT

THE OLD

The SAT, first administered in 1926, has undergone a thorough restructuring. For the last ten years, the SAT consisted of two sections: Verbal and Math. The Verbal section contained Analogies, Sentence Completions, and Critical Reading passages and questions. The Math section tested arithmetic, algebra, and geometry, as well as some probability, statistics, and data interpretation.

You received one point for each correct answer. For most questions, a quarter of a point was deducted for each incorrect answer. This was called the "wrong-answer penalty," which was designed to neutralize random guessing. If you simply filled in the bubble sheet at random, you'd likely get one-fifth of the items correct, given that each item has five answer choices (excluding student-produced–response items). You'd also get four-fifths of the items wrong, losing $4 \times {}^1/_4$, or 1 point for the four incorrectly answered items. Every time you determined an answer choice was wrong, you'd improve your odds by beating the wrong-answer penalty. The net number of points (less wrong-answer penalties) was called the "raw score."

Raw score = # of correct answers – ($^1/_4$ × # of wrong answers)

That score was then converted to the familiar 200–800 "scaled score."

THE NEW

For 2005, the SAT added a Writing section and an essay, changed the name of *Verbal* to *Critical Reading*, and added algebra II content to the Math section. The following chart compares the old SAT with the new SAT:

Old SAT	New SAT
Verbal	**Critical Reading**
Analogies	*Eliminated*
Sentence Completions	Sentence Completions
Long Reading Passages	Long Reading Passages
Paired Reading Passages	Paired Reading Passages
	Short Reading Passages
Math—Question Types	
Multiple Choice	Multiple Choice
Quantitative Comparisons	*Eliminated*
Student-produced Responses	Student-produced Responses
Math—Content Areas	
Numbers & Operations	Numbers & Operations
Algebra I	Algebra I
	Algebra II
Geometry	Geometry
Data Analysis, Statistics & Probability	Data Analysis, Statistics & Probability
	Writing
	Identifying Sentence Errors
	Improving Sentences
	Improving Paragraphs
	Essay
Total Time: 3 hours	*Total Time*: 3 hours, 45 minutes
Maximum Scaled Score: 1600	*Maximum Scaled Score*: 2400 Separate Essay Score (2–12)

The scoring for the test is the same, except that the Writing section provides a third 200–800 scaled score, and there is now a separate essay score. The wrong-answer penalty is still in effect.

NEW PACKAGE, OLD PRODUCT

While the test has changed for test-*takers*, it has not changed all that much from the test-*maker*'s point of view. The Educational Testing Service (ETS) is a not-for-profit institute that creates the SAT for The College Board. Test creation is not as simple a task as you might think. Any standardized test question has to go through a rigorous series of editorial reviews and statistical studies before it can be released to the public. In fact, that's why the old SAT featured a seventh unscored, "experimental" section: new questions were introduced and tested out in these sections. ETS "feeds" potential questions to its test-takers to measure the level of difficulty. Given the complex and lengthy process of developing new questions, it would be impossible for ETS to introduce *totally* new question types or make major changes to existing question types.

Now that you know these facts, the "new" SAT will start to make more sense. The changes were neither random nor unexpected. Actually, the only truly *new* question type on the SAT is the short reading passage followed by a couple of questions. However, the skills tested and strategies required are virtually identical to the tried-and-true long-reading-passage question type. All other additions to the test consist of new *content* rather than new *question types*. Both multiple-choice and student-produced–response math questions ("grid-ins") will now feature algebra II concepts. Same question type, new content. Critical Reading features one fiction passage per test as well as questions on genre, rhetorical devices, and cause and effect. Same question type, different content.

Even the much-feared new Writing section is in a sense old news. The PSAT and the SAT II Writing tests have featured exactly the same multiple-choice question types for years. The essay format and scoring rubric are virtually identical to those of the SAT II Writing test. The College Board had no other choice, given how long the test-development process is.

The other major changes are omissions, not additions: Quantitative Comparisons and Analogies have been dumped from the test.

So, in a nutshell, ETS has simply attached an SAT II Writing test to the old SAT, dropped Analogies and Quantitative Comparisons, added some algebra II content and short reading passages, and ensured that some fiction and fiction-related questions are included. That's it.

A USER'S GUIDE

Reading this book will help expand your vocabulary, which is critical for maximizing your score on the new Critical Reading and Writing sections on the SAT. In this book, we do more than provide you with endless lists of words to memorize: we give you targeted tools for increasing your vocabulary. By mastering the **Power Tactics** in this book, you will build and focus your knowledge in several related areas. You will then have an opportunity to apply what you've just learned on the **Practice Sets**. You'll learn:

- How the SAT actually tests vocabulary knowledge
- The nature of your vocabulary knowledge, and how the SAT doesn't require perfect knowledge to gain points
- How to use knowledge of foreign languages, as well as Greek and Latin word parts, to expand your vocabulary
- How context clues and knowledge of individual words combine to get you points
- Several powerful methods for learning vocabulary words
- How to use a dictionary to build your vocabulary

We present a list of the top 92 SAT vocabulary words, a list of commonly used word roots, and a list of helpful prefixes and suffixes. We then show you how to use these lists to get more points. You can reinforce your new-found vocabulary knowledge with the exercises at the end of this book.

In order to get the most out of this book:

- Make sure to read each section thoroughly and carefully.
- Create flashcards as directed and study them.
- Attempt the exercises only after dedicated study of your flashcards.
- *Enjoy* the Flocabulary at the end of the book!

THE POWER TACTICS

VOCABULARY ON THE NEW SAT

The new SAT places greater importance on testing the meaning of words in the *context* of a sentence, paragraph, or passage. That's why Analogies, the dreaded question type that tested vocabulary knowledge in a vacuum, were dumped for the new version of the SAT. Analogies looked something like this:

2. EVIL : DIABOLICAL ::

(A) good : devilish
(B) good : angelic
(C) bad : beneficent
(D) bad : amoral
(E) immoral : saintly

(The answer, by the way, is **B**; just as a diabolical person does evil, an angelic person does good.)

On the new SAT, your knowledge of vocabulary is now directly tested in the Critical Reading section via **Sentence Completions** and a Reading Passage question type called **Vocabulary-in-Context**. Here's an example of each:

Sentence Completions

3. Recipes for watercolor paint caution against adding too much pigment, lest the paint become -------, resulting in watercolors that are too thick and sticky to work with properly.

(A) translucent
(B) ponderous
(C) malleable
(D) glutinous
(E) vitiated

The answer is **D**; *glutinous* means "having the quality of glue; gummy; sticky."

Reading Passages

The relevant lines of text from the passage are excerpted directly below.

> During his drip-paintings period, Jackson Pollack worked both feverishly and deliberately, flinging paint with abandon, but always according to a loosely preconceived scheme.

4. As used in line 19, "feverishly" most nearly means

(A) sickly
(B) haphazardly
(C) languidly
(D) actively
(E) carefully

The answer is **D**; *feverishly* means "with intense emotion or activity."

In both cases, vocabulary is tested *within sentences*. Context matters and can help you figure out the proper meaning. But context clues are only a part of the story.

ARE CONTEXT CLUES FRIGGLEGARP?

Often, context can help you decipher the meaning of unknown words. Try it in the following exercise:

> While love is necessary for a successful relationship, it is not frigglegarp; other traits such as patience, understanding, and respect must also exist.

What do you think *frigglegarp* means? Well, it might mean something like "sufficient," given the sentence structure.

Now try this one:

> The amount of water provided is frigglegarp to irrigate the field.

How would you know whether *frigglegarp* means "sufficient" or "insufficient" just from the sentence structure? Either meaning could work.

The moral of the story: you need a two-pronged attack. While you will often find that context clues can help you pick up enough of a word's meaning to answer a Sentence Completion or Vocabulary-in-Context question, sometimes you'll just need to know the word, or have some strategies for decoding it on the spot. This book concentrates on building those strategies.

THE TARGET MODEL

If you took a snapshot of your vocabulary knowledge right now, it would look a bit like a target. We call this the **Target Model**:

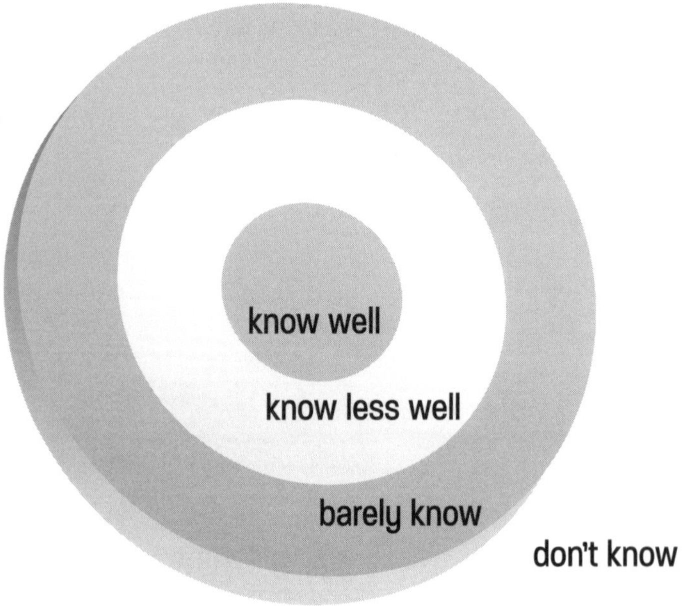

The words you know cold and use all the time are in the center circle. One ring out are the words you know fairly well but rarely use—in other words, you recognize their meanings. The next ring out are words you feel less confident about but that you could probably label as "negative" or "positive" words. Outside the target are all the words you don't know well enough or don't know at all.

The goal is to increase the area of each of the inner target circles. While we do want you to gain as much control over as many words as possible, even partial knowledge can help you eliminate answer choices and gain points on the SAT. Learning words will increase the area of the center circle; learning roots, suffixes, and prefixes will expand the area of the outer circles.

Building your vocabulary will not only help you with Sentence Completions and Vocabulary-in-Context questions. The greater your vocabulary, the quicker and more accurately you'll be able to:

- *Decipher* higher-level meaning in the Critical Reading section's short and long reading passages.
- *Recognize* misused words in the Writing section's multiple-choice questions.
- *Generate* an appropriate and forceful essay.

Finally, what you learn here will apply to your post–SAT life. A large vocabulary helps you communicate more effectively in school, at work, and at home.

ESSENTIAL STRATEGIES

There are a few well-known methods for expanding your vocabulary:

- Studying lists
- Creating flashcards
- Reading well-written prose every day
- Using a dictionary while reading
- Employing vocabulary-building exercises

Going forward, we will familiarize you with all of these methods and provide you with plenty of exercises.

Before we dive in, we want to point out a lesser-known advantage many English-speakers have: knowledge of foreign languages and the related value of knowing Greek and Latin roots, suffixes, and prefixes.

A VERY BRIEF HISTORY OF ENGLISH

Why would knowledge of French, German, or Spanish help with English vocabulary? Why should you bother memorizing Greek and Latin roots, suffixes, and prefixes? The answers to these questions lie in the development of the English language.

Old English broke off from a precursor to German called *Germanic* sometime in the fifth century. At this point, English was just one of many Germanic languages. However, the Latin-speaking Romans had maintained an outpost in England since the first century, so some Latinate words had trickled down into Old English. Over the next few centuries, English gained some more Germanic influence from Viking invasions in the eighth century. But the key event in Old English—the terminal event, actually—was the Norman invasion in 1066.

The Normans spoke an early version of French, a Romance language that had split off from Latin centuries before. Norman French stripped

English of much of its Germanic roots, changing grammar forever and making English the semi-Romance language it is today. For our purposes, the crucial development was that a Latin-by-way-of-early-French vocabulary started to mix in with the older Germanic words. Today English contains many synonym pairs that stem from this mixture:

Germanic	Romance
brotherhood	fraternity
catlike	feline
ask	request
sheep	mutton
ax	hatchet

Middle English began in the twelfth century and continued on into the fifteenth century. During this period the French influence grew, carrying its Latinate vocabulary throughout English society as Normans and Anglo-Saxons intermarried. Modern English began in the sixteenth century and continues on to this day, with Greek and Latin having a significant and direct impact on vocabulary through the rise of science and scientific terminology. English-speakers have long looked to the classical languages when creating *neologisms*—or new words. *Neologism* itself is a perfect example: *neo* means "new"; *logos* means "word."

So, the recipe for English is to:

- Take one part Germanic
- Add one part Romance
- Season liberally with Greek and Latin

Any knowledge of modern-day French, Spanish, Italian, or Portuguese will give you a shot at many of the more complex Latinate English words. Of course, **false friends** dog every language-learner—sometimes identical-looking words in, say, French and English mean different things. For example, you might assume the French word *eventuel* translates as *eventual* in English, but it actually means *possible* or *potential*. However, the general point still holds: knowledge of Romance languages can help you decipher many difficult English words. If you've studied

German, that may be less helpful for vocabulary but not useless. Be on the lookout for similarities. Here are a few examples.

Foreign Language	English Word
Latin	referendum, formula, stimulus
Greek	archetype, hubris, metaphor, sarcasm
French	bandage, caprice, artisan, picturesque
German	kindergarten, leitmotif, zeitgeist
Spanish	armada, cargo, mosquito, cigar
Portuguese	albino, caste, molasses, marmalade
Italian	cupola, extravaganza, fiasco, graffiti, imbroglio

There are also many "near cognates" that have similar but not identical meaning and form. Words are cognates if they derive from a common ancestral language. These, too, can help.

Greek and Latin roots, prefixes, and suffixes are powerful methods for expanding vocabulary. As with *neologism*, many fancy, highfalutin words are no more than Greek and Latin word parts glued together. Given the emphasis on the highfalutin' on the SAT, you'd do well to memorize the most common word parts. We list them for you later on in this book.

REAL SAT WORD LISTS

Word lists have two main advantages: they are easy to find and easy to use. However, each advantage hides a significant disadvantage. We'll examine their *ubiquity* first (yes, that's a good word to look up!). SAT vocabulary lists are everywhere. But most are created simply by reusing a GRE or LSAT list or by simply compiling what seem to be "hard" words the SAT *might* use.

The following list of 92 words is different. It was constructed by counting how many times words appeared on publicly released SAT tests between 1995 and 2002. Our sample consists of words used as answer choices in Analogies, Sentence Completions, and Vocabulary-in-Context items. These 92 words or word groups have appeared at least four times since 1995. While past appearance is no guarantee of future appearance, the following list will at least give you an idea of the level of vocabulary difficulty on recent SAT tests.

We eliminated one major disadvantage to SAT word lists: unlike many—if not most—of the lists out there, ours is based on an actual frequency analysis of recent SAT tests. Unfortunately, we can't help you with the other disadvantages.

Like we said, lists are easy to use. You just cover up one side, and you're off! Use the definitions to name the words or, using the words, provide definitions. What could possibly be wrong with that? Allow us to *list* the many disadvantages.

Why Not to Use Word Lists

1. Lists (including the one following) cannot provide all possible meanings for the words they provide. Only a dictionary can do that, and SAT vocabulary questions often turn on secondary or even *tertiary* (again, a good SAT word!) meanings.
2. When you learn from a list, your memory of the order in which the words appear in the list can interfere with your memorization of their definitions.
3. Furthermore, this "false context" of order is the only one a list can provide. "True contexts," such as "words that all mean 'hatefulness,'" are impossible, since you can't reshuffle a printed list.
4. There's a tendency to look at any list as "everything you could ever possibly need to know," and thus a temptation to *eschew* (look it up!) all other methods for building vocabulary. In that case, you're only as good as your list. Our list is as good as it gets, but it's still only 92 words.
5. Even the best list can only help you learn the words it contains, since you're learning individual words.

Given these disadvantages, we strongly suggest that you do *not* study directly from the following list. We suggest, rather, that you turn this list into the *nucleus* of your flashcard collection. Skim this list quickly: we'll meet you on the other side for a discussion on the great advantages of creating and using flashcards.

Real SAT Vocabulary List

Word or Word Group	Definition
abandoned	*v*: to give oneself up to (e.g., evil); to cast off or reject
accusation (accuse)	*n*: an indictment, a charge of an offense; the act of accusing
ambiguity (ambiguous)	*n*: hesitation, doubt; an uncertainty; an instance of double meaning
analyze (analyst)	*v*: to examine critically in order to bring out key elements or structure; to ascertain the elements of something
antagonize (-ism, -istic, -ist)	*v*: to struggle against
apology (apologize, apologetic)	*n*: an acknowledgment of fault or failure
architect (architecture)	*n*: a designer of any complex structure or plan
astute	*adj*: shrewd, crafty
blueprint	*n*: a plan or program of action
boundary	*n*: something that marks the limit or dividing line, or that limit itself
canvas	*n*: a type of cloth used in sails, tents, to paint on *v*: to solicit support or votes
comic (comedy, comedian)	*adj*: causing or intended to cause laughter
compassion (-ate)	*n*: sympathy, pity
compete (competition, competitive)	*v*: to strive for an objective
complex (complexity)	*n*: a group of related elements *adj*: formed by combination; intricate or not easily analyzed
comprehensive	*adj*: large in scope; all-inclusive

Word or Word Group	Definition
compromise	*n*: a joint agreement between two parties *v*: to come to terms by mutual concessions
condemn (condemnation)	*v*: to declare to be wrong or evil
conflict	*n*: a battle, a fight *v*: to fight or to battle
confusion (confused)	*n*: the state of being perplexed
consensus	*n*: agreement or unity of opinion
contemporary	*adj*: occurring at the same time
contempt (contemptuous)	*n*: the act of despising someone or something
convention (conventional)	*n*: an agreement; a norm or generally accepted rule, practice, or behavior; an assembly of people
conversation	*n*: a spoken interchange; a talk
corrective (correct, correction)	*n*: something that counteracts harm; something that restores health or proper behavior
critic (critical, criticism, criticize)	*n*: one who judges the truth or value of any matter
debate (debatable)	*n*: strife or contention in argument *v*: to argue, discuss, quarrel over
deceit (deceitful, deceive)	*n*: misrepresentation or concealment of the truth; an instance of such behavior
defend	*v*: to protect or uphold
defined (definable, definition)	*adj*: having a specified outline or form
demand	*n*: a request, especially if urgent *v*: to ask for or require
deride	*v*: to laugh mockingly at; to scorn
desert	*v*: to abandon
destroy (destruction)	*v*: to ruin or put out of existence
determined	*adj*: resolved upon; resolute

Word or Word Group	Definition
digress (digression)	*v*: to deviate from or to stray; to depart from the main point in argument
discredit	*n*: a lack of reputation; a loss or lack of confidence or trust *v*: to injure the reputation of; to disbelieve
disease	*n*: illness
disregard	*v*: to pay no attention to
distort (distortion)	*v*: to twist; to misrepresent
document	*v*: to prove by evidence
dominate (dominance, dominant)	*v*: to master; to prevail
doubt (doubtful)	*n*: uncertainty *v*: to hesitate to believe; to be uncertain
elect (election, electorate)	*v*: to choose *n*: chosen, selected
emotion	*n*: a state of mind; a strong feeling
endurance (endure)	*n*: the ability to last or hold out
enhance	*v*: to raise the level of
evaporate (evaporation)	*v*: to convert into gas; to disappear
exclude (exclusive)	*v*: to keep out; to deny entry to
expand (expansion)	*v*: to spread out; to give full expression to
generosity (generous)	*adj*: magnanimity; liberality in giving
hedonism (hedonist, hedonistic)	*n*: the love of pleasure as the chief goal of life
hypocrisy (hypocrite, hypocritical)	*n*: the practice of falsely professing a belief to which one's own actions do not conform
hypothesis	*n*: a proposition or assumption put forth as the basis for further investigation
illusory (illusion)	*adj*: deceptive
imitate (imitation)	*v*: to mimic or copy
integrity	*n*: completeness; free from moral corruption

Word or Word Group	Definition
investigate (investigation, investigator)	*v*: to examine a matter thoroughly; to make a systematic search
isolation (isolated)	*n*: unconnected with anything else
lubricate (lubricant)	*v*: to make slippery or smooth in order to minimize friction
manual	*adj*: pertaining to hands, especially labor done by hand *n*: a book of instruction
measure	*n*: a size or quantity determined by measuring; something assessed by judgment or observation *v*: to ascertain size, quantity, or distance; to regulate or restrain
modest (modesty)	*adj*: having a moderate estimate of one's ability; not exaggerated or excessive
narrate (narrative, narrator)	*v*: to tell a story
navigate (navigable, navigation)	*v*: to find one's way
neglect (negligence, negligent)	*v*: to pay no or insufficient attention to
novel (novelty, novelist)	*v*: new, original *n*: a usually long prose narrative
obey (obedience)	*v*: to comply with or submit to
observe (observable, observation)	*v*: to watch carefully; to adhere to (e.g., a custom)
offense (offensive)	*n*: an attack; a breach of law, duty, or manners
oppose (opponent, opposition)	*v*: to set oneself against; to confront with objections
perplex (perplexing, perplexity)	*v*: to confuse; to torment
persistent (persistence)	*adj*: enduring; persisting in an action

Word or Word Group	Definition
persuade (persuasive)	*v*: to successfully talk someone into an action or belief
plot	*n*: a small piece of ground; a plan; a conspiracy *v*: to plan, especially a conspiracy
preserve	*v*: to keep from harm
progress (progressive)	*n*: advancement; development *v*: to proceed; to move by stages; to move forward
prohibitive (prohibit)	*adj*: having the quality of preventing something from happening
prosaic (prose)	*adj*: commonplace, dull
protagonist	*n*: the chief person in a work of fiction; the leading person in a contest
restrain (restraint, restrained)	*v*: to prevent from doing something; to limit
revise (revision)	*v*: to look over repeatedly, as in a plan or piece of writing
satisfactory (satisfy)	*adj*: sufficient, adequate
scrutinize	*v*: to inspect closely; to examine methodically
stimulate (stimulant, stimulation, stimulus)	*v*: to rouse to action; to animate
supplant	*v*: to cause the downfall of; to remove from a position
suppress	*v*: to cause an activity to cease; to cause a person to become powerless
surreptitious	*adj*: obtained by suppression of the truth; acting stealthily or secretly
universal	*adj*: applicable in all cases; including or affecting all members of a particular group; pertaining to the universe
varied	*adj*: of different sorts or kinds
venerate (venerable, venerability)	*v*: to regard with deep respect; to pay honor to something

FLASHCARD BENEFITS

Flashcards have many benefits. First, they can be shuffled, which not only rids you of the false context of order but also allows you to create piles of words that are related in some way. Learning words in groups tends to increase your chances of remembering them. Some suggestions for grouping: positive words, negative words, words relating to bodies, words of criticism, words of praise, words about abstract ideas, and so forth. Deciding what groups to use is less important than coming up with the groups, reshuffling your piles accordingly, and constantly shifting among the groupings.

Second, the very act of creating flashcards will help you remember words. When you write, you use a different part of your brain than when you read. So, if you both read and write, you have a better shot at memorizing. Furthermore, you can add other meanings to a card. Say you've discovered a second or even third meaning for a particular word, such as *list*. You knew it meant "a written series of items," but you now discover that it can also mean "a deviation from the vertical" or "a tilt."

Third, you can always add to your stock of cards. It might take a while to get all 92 of these words down on cards, but adding, say, twenty a week until test day can be quite manageable. Likewise, these cards will last a long time.

What should your flashcards look like? Here's a model:

Front:

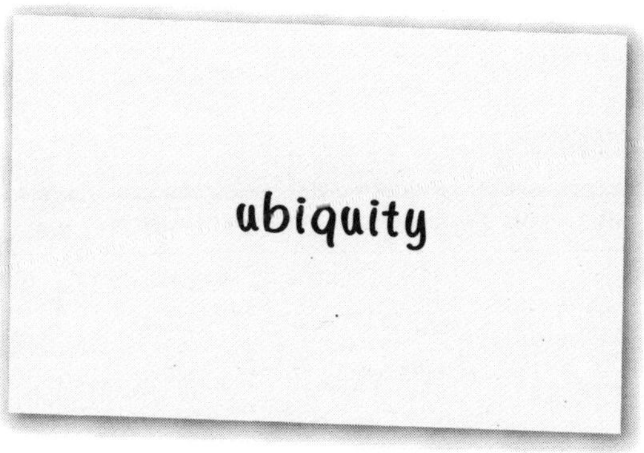

In general, you don't want any other information on the front; be sure not to include anything that might tip you off to the word's meaning.

Back:

> Noun. A presence that is everywhere or in most places simultaneously; omnipresence.
>
> The ring of the cell phone is a ubiquity in contemporary life.
>
> Grouping: Presence/Absence
> ubiquitous

The back is where you want the part of speech, a good definition, and a sample sentence. If you force yourself to use the word correctly in a sentence, or even if you copy down a brief, correct use of the word from elsewhere, you will be reinforcing memorization. Always start writing at the top; you may want to add to this card later.

Also, if you want to list groupings, do so on the back. For example, you could label this card "words of presence/absence." Another useful addition is other forms of the word—what we refer to as the "word group" in the list above. Of course, if the form is different enough in meaning, you should create a separate card for that form. *Self* and *selfishness* should not be on the same card; *ubiquity* and *ubiquitous* certainly can be, as you can see on the card above.

Use 5 × 7 index cards. They're still very portable but leave enough space for additions.

WORD PARTS

Let's take another look at the disadvantages of learning words from lists:

1. Lists cannot provide all possible meanings for the words they provide. Only a dictionary can do that, and SAT vocabulary questions often turn on secondary or even tertiary meanings.
2. When you learn from a list, your memory of the order in which the words appear in the list can interfere with your memorization of their definitions.

3. Furthermore, this "false context" of order is the only one a list can provide. "True contexts," such as "words that all mean *hatefulness*," are impossible, since you can't reshuffle a printed list.
4. There's a tendency to look at any list as "everything you could ever possibly need to know," and thus it's tempting to *eschew* all other methods for building vocabulary. In that case, you're only as good as your list. Our list is as good as it gets, but it's still only 92 words.
5. Even the best list can only help you learn the words it contains, since you're learning individual words.

You've seen how flashcards partially address the first four disadvantages. Flashcards:

---

1. Accommodate fuller primary meanings, as well as secondary and tertiary meanings.
2. Allow for shuffling.
3. Allow for categorization into groups of related words.
4. May be added to without limit.

What about the fifth disadvantage? Even the vaunted word-based flashcard cannot help you there. However, roots, prefixes, and suffixes give you more bang for your buck. What's more efficient, learning one hundred words cold, or learning a few dozen word parts that will give you a decent shot at deciphering the meaning of hundreds of words? Exactly. (For those of you who replied, "Why not do both?" you get a special prize for *prescience*, or perhaps just for *perspicacity*. [Look them up!])

What follows are lists of common Greek and Latin roots, suffixes, and prefixes. Some obvious ones are purposely omitted—you most likely know what the prefix *anti-* means, for example, so you won't see it listed below. Roots are listed in the first chart, prefixes and suffixes together in the second. Some roots also act as prefixes or suffixes, and vice versa; these are only listed once. Skim the charts; we'll meet you on the other side to tell you what to do with them and how they will help you gain points.

Helpful Roots

Root	What It Means	Example
aco(u)	to hear, hearing	acoustic
act, ag	to act, to do, to drive	active, agent

Root	What It Means	Example
agog(ue), agogy	to lead, leader, guiding, inducing	demagogue
agon, agonist	struggle, content	agony, antagonist
alg, algesia, algia	pain	analgesic
am, amat	to love	amiable, amorous
ambul	to walk	circumambulate, amble
andro, andry	male	android, androgynous
anim	mind, feeling, life	animate
anthrop	man, human being	philanthropy, anthropology
aqu	water	aquatic, aquarium
arch	first, ancient, rule	archaic, archive
aud	to hear, hearing, aloud	audible, audience
aug, auct, auth, aux	to increase, to create	augment, author, auxiliary
auto	of, by, for, or in oneself	autobiography, autocrat, autodidact
bene, bon	good	bonus, benefit
brac, brachi	the arm	brachiate, bracelet
cant, cent	to sing	canticle, chant, recant, incantation
cap, capt, cep, cept	box, to take, contain, seize	capture, receipt, capacious

Root	What It Means	Example
capit, capt, cipit	head, chief	capital, precipitate, chapter, capitulate
carn	flesh	carnal, incarnate, carnivore
caus, cuse	to cause	causal, excuse, accuse
ced, cede, ceed, cess	to yield, to go	cede, accessible, necessary
cern, cert, cret, crim	to separate, to distinguish	discern, uncertain
chrom, chromat	color	chromatic, polychromatic
chron	time	synchronous, chronicle
cid, cide	to kill	regicide, suicide, genocide
cis, cise	to cut	excise, scissors
cog, cogit	to think	cognitive, cogent
coll	glue, to stick together	colloquy, collage
corp, cors	body	corporeal, corpulent
cosm	universe, order	cosmic, cosmopolitan
creant, cred, creed	to believe, to trust	credence, credit, incredible
cruc, crus	cross, significant	crux, crusade, crucial
de, div	concerning God or deities	divine, deity
dic, dict, diction	to say, speech, word	dictate, indicate, edict, benediction

Root	What It Means	Example
doc, doct, dog, dox	to teach, learning	doctrine, dogma, orthodox
dom	house, master	domestic, dominate
equ, qui	equal, even	equate, adequate, equinox
esthe, esthesia	to feel, sensation	anesthesia, esthetics
fid, fidel	faith, trust	fidelity, confidence, infidel
fin, finite	end, purpose	infinite, definite
flu, fluor, flux, fluv	to flow	affluence, fluid, superfluous
for, fort	strong	fortress, enforce, comfort
fract, frag, frang, fring	to shatter	fracture, fragment, fragile, refract
gen, gon	birth, race, kind	genetic, gonad, congenital, gender
ger, gest	to carry, to produce	gestate, gesture, digest
grad, grade, gress	to step, a degree or grade	gradual, degree, progress
gram, graph	a written record, to write	telegram, autograph
grat	pleasing, thankful	gratitude, congratulate, ingratiate
greg	society, group	aggregate, gregarious
gynec, gyn, gynist	female	gynecologist, misogyny

Root	What It Means	Example
hier, hieratic	holy, sacred	hierarchy, hieroglyphic
hol	whole	holistic, hologram
hydr, hydro	water, liquid	hydraulics, hydrant
ideo	idea, philosophy	ideology, idol, ideal
idi, idio	personal, private	idiosyncratic, idiom
iso	equal, similar	isometric, isotope
ject, jet	to throw	eject, inject, jettison, projectile
jud, jur, just	right, law	jury, judgment, judicious, injury, perjury
jug, junct	a link, to join	juncture, conjunction, conjugate
kine, kinesia, kinesis	movement, energy	kinetic, cinema
lat, late, lation	to bear, to carry	collate, correlate, legislate, translate
lect, leg, lig	to choose, to read	legible, intelligent, dialect, collect
lev, lieve, life	to lift, light in weight	alleviate, elevator, relief
lign, line	line	delineate, lineage
locut, loqu, loquy	to speak, speech	locution, circumlocution, eloquent, ventriloquist
log, logue, logy, lexico	speech, word, study of	logic, lecture, analogy

Root	What It Means	Example
luc, lumin, lux	light, to shine	illuminate, lucent, luminary, elucidate
macro	large	macrocosm
mal	bad	malady, malcontent, malefactor
medi, meso, mid	in the middle of	intermediate, mediocre, medium
micro	small	microscope
mis	hate	misanthrope, misogyny
mor, mort	death	mortal, mortician, mortify
neg	to deny	negate, neglect, renege
neo	new	neologism, neonate
noct, nox	night	nocturnal, equinox
nom, num	law	nomad, economy, astronomy
od, odia	smell	odor, odious
opt, optic	eye, vision	panopticon, optics,
ov, ovul	egg, egg-shaped	oval, ovulate
par, pare	equal	pair, parity, peer, compare
part, patri	father	patriot, patronage, patriarch, paternal
path, pathic, pathy	emotion, suffering	pathological, pathetic, sympathy, empathy
pel, puls	to drive, driven	pulse, compulsion, expel, impulse

Root	What It Means	Example
phil, philia	love, fondness for	philosophy, philanthropy, philander, philology
phob, phobo	fear	phobia
plaud, plaus, plod, plos	to make a loud noise	applaud, explode
plen, plet	to fill, full	plentiful, plethora, replenish
prim, prin	first	primary, primate, premier
pur, purg	to clear of guilt, to get rid of something unwanted	purge, pure, expurgate, purgatory
quest, quir, quisit	to ask	request, inquest, question, acquire, conquer
qui, quil, quit	rest	quiet, quit, acquiesce, acquit
rad, radic	root	radical, eradicate
rati, reas	to think, calculate	rate, ratify, rational, reasonable
rect, reg, rig	to rule or guide, proper, straight	rectify, regal, region, regulate, rigorous
rupt	to break, to sever	rupture, abrupt, disrupt, corrupt, interrupt
salu, salv	safety, health	salubrious, salvage, salutary
scrib, scribe, script	to write, something written	circumscribe, ascribe, describe, inscribe, prescribe

Root	What It Means	Example
secut, sequ	to follow, to ensue	sequence, consequence, execute, consecutive
sen, senil	old, old age	senior, senator, senescence
ser, sor	a series, attachment	serial, desert, assert
solute, solv	to release, to loosen, to free	dissolve, absolute, insoluble
soph, sophy	wisdom	philosophy, sophisticated
spec, spect, spic	to look, to see	aspect, specific, spectator, spectrum, specimen
spir, spire	to breathe, breath, spirit	aspire, expire, conspire, transpire
stant, stat, stit	to stand, to stay, to state	assistant, consistent, constant, status, stance, destiny
stru, struct	to build, a building or pattern	destructive, instruct, obstruct, structural
tact, tang, teg, ting	to touch	tactile, taste, tangible, contact, contingent
temper, tempor, temp	time, balance	temporize, temporary, contemplate, temperature
ten, tain, tent, tin	to hold	tenable, tenacious, tenet, contain, detain
tend, tens	to stretch	extend, distend, tension, tendril
top, tope, topy	place	topic, topology, utopia

Root	What It Means	Example
tract, treat	to draw, to extend, to attract	extract, treatise, contract, retreat, subtract
trib, tribe, trit	to rub, to wear down	tribulation, trite, attrition
trop, tropic, tropy	to turn, a change or turn	trope, tropic, entropy
troub, turb	confusion, whirling	disturb, perturb, turbine, turbulence
vac, van, vast, void	empty, desolate	vacuum, vacant, vanity, devastate, avoid
vail, val	to be strong, to be worthy	valiant, valor, validate, valence
ver, veri	true	veracious, verdict, verify
vit, viv	life, to live	vital, survive, viable, vivify
voc, vok, vow	voice, to call or summon	vocalize, vociferous, avow, equivocate
vol	will, desire, wish	volition, volunteer, involuntary
vor, vorous, vour	to eat, to swallow	voracious, carnivorous
xene, xeno, xeny	foreign	xenophobe, xenogamy
zoa, zo, zoo, zoon	life, living	zoo, zodiac, metazoan

Helpful Prefixes and Suffixes

Prefix or Suffix	What It Means	Example
a, an	not, without	apathy, analgesic
ab, abs	away, from, separated	abdicate, abort
ac, ad	to, toward	acclaim, accrete, adhere, adjoin
ambi, amphi	both, around	ambiguous, ambidextrous, ambiance
ante, anter	before, prior, in front of	antebellum, antechamber, anterior, antique
ap, apo	away from, detached	apology, apostate, apostle
cata, cat, cath	downwards, against, contrary to	cataclysm, catapult, catharsis
circum	around	circumscribe, circumspect, circumference
co, com, con	with, together	cohabitation, comfort, collude, colloquy
contra	against	contradict, contrast
de	down from, reverse, remove, out of, derived from	decapitate, declare, deface, delegate, delineate
di, dif, dis	separation	disable, dispute, decrease, divert
dys	bad, difficult	dysentery, dysphoria
ec, ecto, ex	outside of, external, away from	eclectic, ecstasy, excursion, excuse, explode
em, en, ent	in, into, within	encourage, endemic, embryo, embargo, enchant
epi	over, above, around	epilogue, epitome, epidemic
eu, ev	well, good	euphoria, eulogy, euphemism
hyper	more, beyond normal, excessive	hyperkinetic, hypersonic
hypo	less, under, below	hypochondria, hypothesis

Prefix or Suffix	**What It Means**	**Example**
in, im, em, en	in, on, amongst, within	incarnate, insert, inspire, instruct, immolate, employ, enchant
in, im	not	immeasurable, improper, inadequate
men, ment	result, means of or product of an action	instrument, ailment, compartment, entanglement
meta, meth	after, along with, transfer, changed	metabolism, metaphor, metaphysics, method
mis	worse, badly	mischief, misadventure, mistake
ob, of, op	toward, against, face-to-face	object, obnoxious, occupy, oppose
par, para	beside, near, faulty	paradox, parasite, parody
per	through, thoroughly	perceive, permit, perpetrate, persuade
peri	around, near, beside	perimeter, peripheral
pre	before, in front of	precept, precede, prediction, predominant, pregnant
pro	earlier, before, forward	proclivity, pronounce, propose
re	back, backwards	recant, recount, recur
se	aside, away	secede, seclude, sever
syl, sym, syn	united, together with, same	synonym, sympathy, syllogism
tra, trans	beyond, across, through	transact, traverse, transport
un	not	unable, undeniable, undone

Okay, now what do you do with these lists?

First: make them into flashcards. Any example word you don't know should be added to your word flashcards.

Second: memorize them.

Third: use them in the following exercises. Your flashcards should look like this:

Front:

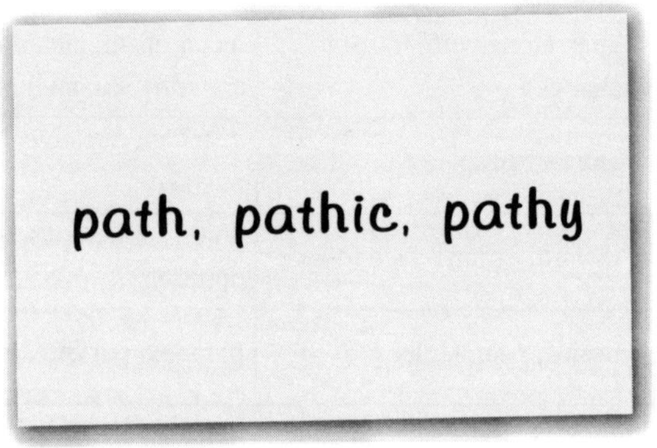

Back:

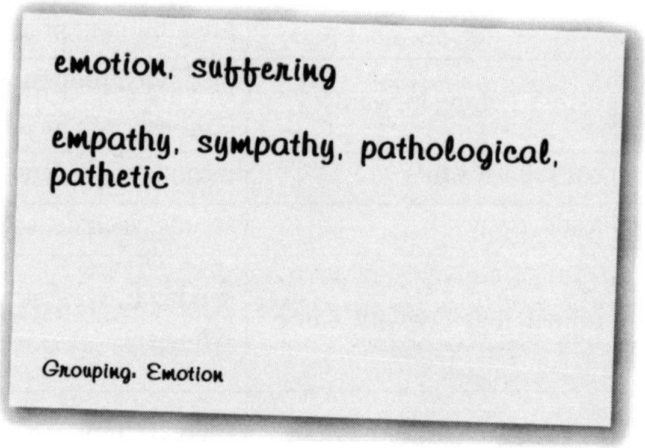

The back of your flashcards should include a definition for each root, example words, and a word-grouping.

Remember the Target Model?

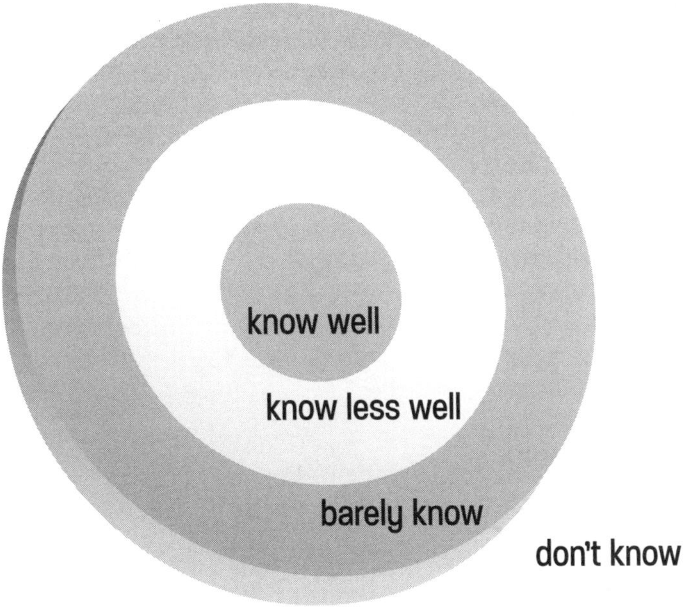

Studying word flashcards will help you expand the "know well" circle. However, you can gain a lot of points with less certain knowledge. If you know you need a "positive" word in a Sentence Completion, you can eliminate any "negative" words in the answer choices. Say you need a word that has something to do with the human body. Well, you can look for the root *corp*; if any answer choice contains that root, there's a very good chance that's your word. You may not be able to define it, but "barely know" can equal a point on the SAT. This is where knowledge of word parts (and of foreign languages) will give you an advantage. Word parts expand the outer circles of the target.

READING AND DICTIONARY USE

You'll need a good dictionary in order to:

- Flesh out your 92 word flashcard definitions
- Create new word flashcards
- Create new word-part flashcards (a good dictionary contains entries for roots, suffixes, and prefixes)

You'll also need to use a good dictionary in conjunction with the last and least painful method for building vocabulary: reading.

Everyone has interests. Somewhere, either online or in print form, you can find well-written prose on your topic of interest. Some suggested sources for good prose include the *New York Times*, the *Washington Post*, *Harper's*, the *Atlantic Monthly*, the *Nation*, the *Economist*, and the *Wall Street Journal*. Make sure you read a little bit every day, whether for schoolwork, for pleasure, or just for SAT preparation. Get in the habit of noting all unfamiliar words. Try to work out their meaning through context clues, word parts, or your knowledge of foreign languages. But don't stop there: at the end of every day (if you have an iron will) or every week (if you're like the rest of us), look these words up in the dictionary and make new flashcards for them. Take every opportunity to lock down the meanings of unfamiliar words. This can and should be the beginning of a lifelong practice that will enrich your life.

What makes for a good dictionary? Here's a good rule of thumb: if the dictionary is big enough to act as a doorstop, you're probably okay. Two suggestions: the *American Heritage College Dictionary* and *Merriam-Webster's Collegiate Dictionary*. For those who want the near-ultimate, purchase the *New Shorter Oxford English Dictionary* as a book or on CD-ROM. The ultimate is the multivolume (or multidisc) *Oxford English Dictionary*, which costs hundreds of dollars and is definitely overkill for SAT preparation. The *OED* is catnip to *philologists*—can you figure out the meaning of this word from the lists above? The more words a dictionary has, and the more it has to say about each word, the better it is.

TIPS AND SELF-GUIDED PRACTICE

Here are some more ways you can enhance your vocabulary knowledge on your own.

1. As you work through practice SAT tests, make sure you circle all unfamiliar words. Try to decipher them through context clues, word parts, and your knowledge of foreign languages, and use your dictionary to find their meanings. Make a flashcard for each word.
2. When you begin using your flashcards, don't worry too much about shuffling them. Group them according to categories you learned in this book or by others that make sense to you. The piles should contain no more than twenty cards. Take advantage of the "false context" of order and start to nail down meanings. Every time you

get a word right, separate it from the pile; every time you get one wrong, leave it in the pile. This way, you'll zero in on the tough ones. When you can provide the meaning of each word in your small pile, shuffle them and retest yourself.

3. Once every couple of weeks, mix up all your cards, shuffle, and test your knowledge of all or a very significant chunk of them. Use between fifty and one hundred cards in each "run."
4. You may find *mnemonics* (pronounced *ni-'mä-niks*) helpful for especially difficult words. In this context, a mnemonic is some kind of phrase that helps you remember the meaning of a word. Often they are anagrams, such as "Please excuse my dear Aunt Sally"—the first letter of each word in this case is used to recall the order of operations in math:

Please: Parentheses
Excuse: Exponents
My: Multiplication
Dear: Division
Aunt: Addition
Sally: Subtraction

Here's an example of a mnemonic the author used to memorize the word *ambidextrous* in his younger, basketball-playing days. As a play on words, the author renamed the word "ambi-dextrose" and defined it as "sweet from either side."

Huh?

Well, here's how the mnemonic worked:

---

1. Dextrose is a type of sugar
2. In basketball, if you can drive the lane successfully from either side—leading with your right or left hand interchangeably—you become very hard to defend.
3. If you could drive the lane from either side, you were *sweet* in the playground slang of the day.
4. *Sweet* led back to *dextrose*; *either side* led back to *ambi*; and to top it all off, if you were able to dribble equally well with either hand, you were, by definition, *ambidextrous*.

As you can see, mnemonics are idiosyncratic, personal, and poetic. This process is a two-edged sword. If your mnemonic quickly leads you to the proper meaning of the word, use it. If it does not lead you quickly to the proper meaning, don't use it.

WHAT'S NEXT?

Once you've converted the preceding lists of words and word parts into flashcards, spend some time studying them. **Don't** just dive into the exercises without having spent several hours learning the words and word parts—save them for self-testing and reinforcement.

Good luck!

THE PRACTICE SETS

WORD EXERCISES

The words used in these exercises are from the list of 92 words that you have made into flashcards and studied. If you haven't done this yet, please stop and do so now. Save these exercises for reinforcement, which is their best use. Answers to these exercises can be found on page 53.

Sometimes an associated word from the word group is used; sometimes a secondary or tertiary meaning not listed in the definition column is used. Consult your dictionary and update your flashcards accordingly if necessary.

MATCHING

Match each word with its definition. In some sets there are more words than definitions; in others, there are more definitions than words.

Set 1

___ 1. novelty	A. causing laughter
___ 2. competitive	B. desiring to strive for an objective
___ 3. imitate	C. despising someone or something
___ 4. apologetic	D. to abandon
___ 5. comic	E. a state of mind; a strong feeling
___ 6. contemptuous	F. something new or unusual
___ 7. desert	G. regretfully acknowledging fault or failure
___ 8. emotion	H. to ruin or put out of existence
___ 9. destroy	

Set 2

___ 1. disregard	A. something that marks the limit or dividing line
___ 2. debatable	B. commonplace; dull
___ 3. prosaic	C. an instance of double meaning
___ 4. suppress	D. marked by actively expressed opposition
___ 5. ambiguity	E. sympathy; pity
___ 6. antagonistic	F. something that restores health

7.	boundary	G.	to cause a person to become powerless
8.	consensus	H.	open to dispute
9.	corrective	I.	to pay no attention to
		J.	unity of opinion

Set 3

1.	deride	A.	to regard with deep respect
2.	electorate	B.	love of pleasure
3.	hedonism	C.	failure to exercise care
4.	lubricant	D.	to confuse
5.	negligence	E.	something that minimizes friction
6.	perplex	F.	acting stealthily or secretly
7.	venerate	G.	a body of people entitled to vote
8.	surreptitious		

Set 4

1.	scrutinize	A.	to examine methodically
2.	stimulus	B.	the chief person in a work of fiction
3.	protagonist	C.	something that animates
4.	integrity	D.	a proposition put forward as the basis for further investigation
5.	hypothesis	E.	deceptive
6.	illusory	F.	to plan, especially a conspiracy
7.	persuasive	G.	a designer of a complex plan
8.	plot	H.	a plan or program of action
9.	architect	I.	having a specified outline or form
10.	blueprint	J.	free from moral corruption
		K.	tending to successfully convince someone of an action or belief

FILL IN THE BLANK

Provide the word that best completes the following sentences.

Set 1

1. Hardly the saint depicted in the textbooks, Lincoln's ________ handling of the election of 1864 shows how shrewd a politician he could be.
2. There will always be those who consider a mere ________ sufficient to prove guilt.

3. The SAT has increasingly tested vocabulary knowledge in context, rather than in ________.
4. The cost of many classroom-based SAT courses is ________; only the well-off can afford such an investment.
5. One of the joys of reading Jonathan Swift's *Gulliver's Travels* is the constant ________ from the main narrative flow.
6. Resistance to study often ________ when students are presented with concrete goals and rewards.
7. A ________ and complicated problem usually requires a proportionally thorough and ________ solution.
8. Wagner and Brahms were close ________; they jointly dominated nineteenth-century classical music.
9. Far from being arrogant, Juanita had a ________ estimate of her own abilities.
10. The greater part of language-learning consists of absorbing agreed-upon ________ that reflect long-standing use rather than consciously memorizing abstract rules.
11. On formal occasions, it's wise to ________ all the social niceties.
12. ________ and ________ are the two poles in public life—there are always those who want to encourage strife and those who desire to end it.
13. Given the sensitivity of the issues being discussed at the conference, any seemingly friendly ________ runs the risk of igniting a fiery ________.
14. Between the unvarnished truth and the bold-faced lie you'll find many gradations, from the merely ________, in which meaning can't be pinned down, to the ________, where meaning is twisted, to the ________ where meaning is deliberately hidden.
15. "I'd like to hear more about that; could you ________ upon your last point?"

Set 2

1. In refusing to respond to the bullies' taunts and insults, the little boy displayed considerable ________ for one so young.
2. The commander was convinced of the strategic importance of capturing the city, but his ________ colleagues and he were unable to reach a ________ on the matter.
3. The incumbent's record on environmental protection was so strong that no other candidate dared to ________ her on the issue.
4. The hastily prepared meal was enough to ________ the gourmand's hunger, but it fell far short of his culinary expectations.

5. Having no further use for the broken toy, the child ________ it in favor of her shiny new tricycle.
6. Determined to help remove the present administration from office, the activists ________ the neighborhood in an effort to garner support for their candidate.
7. The woman's ________ for the sick cannot be questioned; she is a dedicated hospital volunteer and is considering a second career in nursing.
8. The amateur photographer was disappointed in her first attempt at processing film; the colors were dull and the figures lacked ________.
9. The college freshman found that maintaining an A-average, a spot on the varsity team, and an active social life ________ careful use of both time and energy.
10. ________ to secure high political office, Lyndon Johnson would often campaign during bouts of sometimes life-threatening illness to obtain popular support.
11. The boy attempted to ________ his neighborhood rival by placing the blame for the broken window on him.
12. Because the ________ was diagnosed at an early stage, the patient was able to receive timely treatment and make a full recovery.
13. Prior to meeting with the company president, Lisa collected past and present sales data to ________ her division's improved performance.
14. The team's ________ over the sport of baseball is evident in its accumulation of recent championship titles.
15. To the great surprise of his rescuers, the injured camper ________ several days with little water and no food.
16. Those who preach about the value of a hard day's work but who have never performed one are guilty of ________.
17. Knitting, a textile craft thought to have originated in ancient Egypt, requires considerable ________ dexterity.
18. The monotonous hum of the shop-floor machinery began early in the morning and ________ late into the night.
19. The ________ children did as their parents requested, completing their chores and homework before going to their beds.
20. Vanity, jealousy, and pride are ________ emotions that affect all humans, regardless of race, culture, or nationality.
21. The cake recipe called for equal ________ of flour and sugar.
22. Orson Welles, the renowned actor, director, and screenwriter, also provided ________ and voice-overs for radio story-hours, commercials, and documentaries.

23. The young man ________ the elderly woman's sense of religious etiquette by failing to remove his hat upon entering the church.
24. The ecologist has received many awards for his work in ________ the natural habitat of endangered species.
25. The glassworks of Louis Tiffany are praised for their intricate Art Nouveau designs and ________ colors ranging from deepest blue to palest pink.
26. Captured and ________ by the invading forces, the former king had little choice but to remain locked in the dungeons while his enemies determined his fate.

FILL-IN-THE-BLANK ESSAYS

Read each essay and supply the best word from your flashcards for each of the blanks. Words are used only once; each blank requires a unique word.

Set 1

"I have ________ that which no man has yet withstood: I have kissed the hands that murdered my son."

Achilles, Greek paragon of war, gazed in wonder at the kneeling king of Troy . . . and then in equal wonder at his own mighty hands, hands that had ripped Prince Hector's life from his body. How many others had suffered the same fate at these hands?

But even as King Priam's noble act of supplication thrust a spear at Achilles' rage, that rage parried. Had not Hector killed his beloved friend Patroclus? Had not Hector stripped Patroclus of Achilles' armor and worn it as his own? Outrageous! He was right to ________ such an insolent ________. He was right to drag Hector's bloody corpse back to the tent in which Hector's father now begged for the chance to show *honor* to that corpse! To have done anything less to that murderous prince would have ________ Patroclus's spirit. Anything less would have shown complete ________ for the vengeance and honor *his* beloved friend deserved. Anything less would have been a ________ denial of Achilles' warrior code, of his personal ________. In fact, perhaps he had not done *enough* to Hector to avenge his friend. He should have eaten Hector's flesh raw—the gods themselves would have deemed it just! Achilles glanced at his sword, eyes ablaze, rage again to the fore, hands itching to hew this _______ king's head from its body. How foolish he had been to have _______ for this sonless king, how _______ was this weak king's supplication!

He met Priam's gaze . . . and hesitated. _______ had once more crept past the sentries that had always protected Achilles' implacable honor. He watched as Priam's eyes overflowed. Tears of loss mingled with tears of rage, but those tears were _______ by nobility. In Priam's eyes, godlike Achilles caught a first fleeting glimpse of himself. In a flash, he grasped Priam's superiority. Could Achilles have acted thus if a son of his had been killed? Would love for his own son have overcome his rage against his son's killer? As he gazed at Priam, Achilles' thoughts flew to his own father, far away, who, like Priam, was never to see his most beloved son again. For Achilles had chosen to follow Hector into death and glory. Achilles' rage and contempt _____________ into the night air, replaced by _______ for this most majestic of kings. He had finally met an _______ over whom he could not triumph. Achilles, for the first time in his life, and with great relief, submitted. He _______ the old king's actions, dropping to his knees and embracing Priam, tearfully promising to _______ the king's wishes.

For a long time, Achilles wept with the king. He wept for Priam's son, for his own father, and for all sons and fathers. Above all, he wept for the needless losses our rage inflicts upon one another, and upon ourselves.

Set 2

How do living cells ________ the energy they need? Inside living cells are specific structures, called *organelles,* that provide the energy necessary for life. In plants, *chloroplasts* trap sunlight and use its energy to create energy-carrying molecules. In animals, *mitochondria* create the same energy-carrying molecules, called *ATP*, by using oxygen to break down ________ organic compounds into carbon dioxide and water. Mitochondria and chloroplasts are about the same size and have the same biochemistry as bacteria. They even have their own DNA ________ and divide within the cell on their own schedule. Bacteria are known as *prokaryotic* cells because they lack most organelles. The more complex cells found in animals and plants are called *eukaryotic* cells; they contain many organelles. One of the most fascinating ________ to come out of biology in the last half century is that these key structures inside the cells of all multicellular life forms were once free-living organisms. This notion is called *endosymbiosis*.

In endosymbiosis, a "guest" and a "host" species coevolve to the point of fusion—the guest species is absorbed into a host species and spends its entire life cycle within the host. The arrangement is not parasitic: one or both of the species benefits. So, how did the precursors to eukaryotic cells acquire mitochondria- and chloroplast-like prokaryotes? In what manner could a microorganism's bodily ________ be breached? The evolutionary ________ has been reconstructed as follows: the story goes that amoeba-like precursors to eukaryotic cells assimilated all kinds of prokaryotic organisms. Most were simply broken down and absorbed, but some hardy proto-organelle organisms survived—even flourished—in the new, nutrient-rich environment.

This hypothesis can never be conclusively proven, but its plausibility has been increasingly ________ as various lines of evidence and ________ have been recorded and conclusions have converged. If true, the endosymbiotic origin of mitochondria and chloroplasts ________, or at least challenges, two long-held tenets. First, we are used to seeing bacterial invasions as just that—causes of disease that constrict life functions. These ancient and ________ guest species have actually radically ________ their hosts' evolutionary horizons. Ironically, we owe our very existence to endosymbiosis. Aside from ________ the development of ever more complex organisms, endosymbiosis solved a critical issue for life on Earth—the increase in oxygen levels. Early life was entirely anaerobic, meaning energy was created without oxygen. In fact, oxygen was the by-product. Oxygen, ________ as it may seem, is actually a poison. This highly reactive element effectively ________ the emergence of terrestrial life. But oxygen-eating proto-mitochondria filled the niche, creating an alternative energy source for their new hosts. Thus, the inclusion of these guest species into the architecture of the eukaryotic cell made complex terrestrial life possible.

Second, since all plants and animals feature these once free-living organelles, the ________ of endosymbiosis challenges our notion of what we take to be an individual organism. The boundaries between self and environment and between individual and colony can seem ________ when one takes the long view of endosymbiosis. Inside our trillions of cells, we carry opportunistic little creatures whose energetic surplus fuels all the varied activities of plants and animals, from the creation of the wood pulp from which the book you're holding was manufactured to the operation of the brain that is now puzzling over this vocabulary-building exercise. So take a deep breath, and reward your oxygen-hungry mitochondria with a well-deserved treat!

Set 3

That all buildings embody the belief systems of the cultures that built them is beyond ________. However, not all buildings are equal. Some are ________ more by functions common to all societies rather than by those culturally specific functions that are central to an entire belief system. For example, modern-day takeout restaurants in New York City look remarkably similar to Roman takeout restaurants still preserved at Pompeii—an L-shaped bar featuring holes for hot pots. Classic architectural monuments stand out because they provide an impressively ________ and immensely complex structural manifestation of the function that reflects, or even ________, a culture. Size and scale also help to denote a classic building: if you want to look closely at what a culture's priorities were, ________ the structure that required the highest investment of ingenuity, resources, and political power. The heart of a culture lies in its greatest buildings.

One such building is the Hagia (pronounced *Hi-ya*) Sophia, the Great Church of the Holy Wisdom, in Istanbul. Istanbul was once known as Constantinople—the City of Constantine, built as a new capital by the Roman emperor who had made Christianity the state religion in the fourth century A.D. Two centuries later, the western Roman empire had fallen, but the eastern empire—known to historians as the Byzantine Empire—had not merely ________, but was in the process of temporarily reconquering the western lands that were once Roman. Justinian, who reigned from 527 to 565, was the ________ of this territorial expansion, which was seen by ________ as restoring the glory and power of the Roman Empire. The restoration was not merely military; Justinian also ordered the codification and clarification of all Roman law as a new, rational basis for civil order. The "Justinian Code" served as the foundation for modern-day law in most European countries.

The restoration of the glory that was Rome can also be seen in Justinian's signature building, the Hagia Sophia. After a riot that destroyed the original Hagia Sophia, and which nearly ________ him, Justinian marshaled a tremendous effort to adapt secular Roman architecture to a new kind of building that epitomized Byzantine power. Unlike most pagan temples, which served mostly as a holy backdrop for outdoor ritual, the Hagia Sophia fused a unique Roman temple—the Pantheon, or "Temple of All the Gods"—with a typical secular building: the basilica, a long, rectangular hall used for law courts or markets. The Pantheon, built by the emperor Hadrian in the early second-century A.D., featured a huge dome resting on a cylindrical drum. At the apex of the dome was a large hole, the oculus, which provided the only natural light. The ________ of the disc of light from the oculus across the floor and walls of the building served to animate this architectural representation of the ordered Roman universe.

Hagia Sophia's dome rested not on a drum, but, radically, on a perfect square. To get from square walls to a circular dome, the Byzantines invented *pendentives*, curving, concave triangular forms that rise from the corners of the cube and spread toward each other, allowing for the transition from cube to hemisphere by rounding off the corners of the cube. The sides of the cube rise toward the base of the dome, progressively rounded off by the ________ pendentives rising from the corners until the gravestone-like curved apex touches the base of the dome. The base of the dome itself—where the four pendentives finally intersect—is punctuated by a series of windows. Hagia Sophia's dome seems to float above the building, "as though suspended from Heaven by a golden chain," as one contemporary observer put it. Arrayed around that dome-on-a-cube was a larger complex of vaulted aisles, half-domes, and upper galleries, all of which opened upward, complementing the immense central space under the dome.

Why did Justinian's architects risk putting a dome on a perfect square? No one had ever attempted this—and despite Justinian's announcement that he had surpassed Solomon as a builder, the dome fell not once but three times in the subsequent 1,500 years, first collapsing a mere thirty years after completion. The answer lies in the near-________ use of large religious buildings to identify imperial power structures with the Divine. Byzantine religious practice, and the central relation between that practice and Byzantine state power, ________ that a Roman dome be placed on a Roman basilica. The patriarch (the leader of the Byzantine church) and the emperor were seen as the two halves of the earthly manifestation of God himself, united in leading an ordered, divinely sanctioned society. Byzantine Christianity purposely cultivated the "Great Mystery" of faith, to which only the patriarch and the emperor were privy. All faith was mediated through these two figures via an elaborate set of rituals, just as all political power was mediated through a Byzantine court bureaucracy so complicated and convoluted that *Byzantine* entered our language as an adjective meaning "of labyrinthine ________."

Citizens crowded into the Hagia Sophia to view elaborate, half-hidden rituals. Only the emperor, the patriarch, and their attendants could walk beneath the dome in the central open space. All others were packed into the aisles and galleries on the periphery, with purposely half-obscured views of the proceedings. That is why Byzantine churches adopted the rectangular basilica—they appropriated the Roman form that was designed to accommodate the multitudes. Not only were the rituals semi-hidden, but full appreciation of the interior domed space of the Hagia Sophia was denied to anyone viewing it from the periphery—which meant everyone but the uppermost elite of the political system. Since that interior space was itself meant to be an architectural representation of Creation, full appreciation of Hagia Sophia's interior space meant full apprehension of Creation itself, a privilege granted only to the elite, and on which the legitimacy of its power rested. Like the Pantheon, the Hagia Sophia was designed to show that the divinely ordered universe was reflected by and embodied in the political structure of society. The implication was purposeful—the political structure was thus sanctioned by Heaven itself. ________ to the regime was the ________ not only of one's loyalty but also of one's piety. Any and all ________ to the regime was thus evil.

Set 4

Many students either ________ the SAT, refusing to have anything to do with such a misguided—even evil—test, or merely ________ it, assuming that by refusing to pay attention, the nasty test will just go away. I believe that fear causes these two reactions.

In order to test this proposition—or, in other words to ________ this ________—we need to thoroughly ________ a current misunderstanding of tests like the SAT. While it is true that the SAT stemmed from the intelligence-testing wing of applied psychology eighty years ago, it is no longer accurate to characterize the SAT as a ________ and anachronistic manifestation of controversial IQ testing. The one clear trend in SAT history is a continual, ________ retreat from "puzzle-solving" item types in all tested areas. However, decades of welcome ________ to the SAT's IQ-testing background have yet to ________ many, if not most, of the public. Furthermore, many of those who ________ the SAT in the media seem to agree with the test's detractors, holding to the ________ that the test measures "intelligence," whatever *that* may be. Thus, students are forced to confront a ________ image of the SAT in which a test designed to ________ the achievement of acquired skills and knowledge becomes a nefarious ________ to ________ the unintelligent from the rewards due to the ________.

ANSWERS TO WORD EXERCISES

Matching

Set 1

1. F
2. B
3. [none]
4. G
5. A
6. C
7. D
8. E
9. H

Set 2

1. I
2. H
3. B
4. G
5. C
6. D
7. A
8. J
9. F

Set 3

1. [none]
2. G
3. B
4. E
5. C
6. D
7. A
8. F

Set 4

1. A
2. C
3. B
4. J
5. D
6. E
7. K
8. F
9. G
10. H

Fill in the Blank

Set 1

1. astute
2. accusation
3. isolation
4. prohibitive
5. digression
6. evaporates
7. complex; comprehensive
8. contemporaries
9. modest
10. conventions
11. observe
12. conflict; compromise
13. conversation; debate
14. ambiguous; distorted; deceitful
15. expand

Set 2

1. restraint
2. doubtful; consensus
3. oppose
4. satisfy
5. abandoned
6. canvassed
7. compassion
8. definition
9. demanded
10. determined
11. discredit
12. disease
13. document
14. dominance
15. endured
16. hypocrisy
17. manual
18. persisted
19. obedient
20. universal
21. measures
22. narration
23. offended
24. preserving
25. varied
26. supplanted

Fill-in-the-Blank Essays

We have tried to ensure that there are no alternative ways to complete this essay. If you think you have a better word for a given blank, please compare your words with those below to ensure that you not only fully understand their definitions but have also used the words correctly given the context of the essay.

Set 1

"I have **endured** that which no man has yet withstood: I have kissed the hands that murdered my son."

Achilles, Greek paragon of war, gazed in wonder at the kneeling king of Troy . . . and then in equal wonder at his own mighty hands, hands that had ripped Prince Hector's life from his body. How many others had suffered the same fate at these hands?

But even as King Priam's noble act of supplication thrust a spear at Achilles' rage, that rage parried. Had not Hector killed his beloved friend Patroclus? Had not Hector stripped Patroclus of Achilles' armor and worn it as his own? Outrageous! He was right to **destroy** such an insolent **antagonist**. He was right to drag Hector's bloody corpse back to the tent in which Hector's father now begged for the chance to show *honor* to that corpse! To have done anything less to that murderous prince would have **offended** Patroclus's spirit. Anything less would have shown complete **disregard** for the vengeance and honor *his* beloved friend deserved. Anything less would have been a **hypocritical** denial of Achilles' warrior code, of his personal **integrity**. In fact, perhaps he had not done *enough* to Hector to avenge his friend. He should have eaten Hector's flesh raw—the gods themselves would have deemed it just! Achilles glanced at his sword, eyes ablaze, rage again to the fore, hands itching to hew this **accusing** king's head from its body. How foolish he had been to have **compassion** for this sonless king, how **contemptible** was this weak king's supplication!

He met Priam's gaze . . . and hesitated. **Doubt** had once more crept past the sentries that had always protected Achilles' implacable honor. He watched as Priam's eyes overflowed. Tears of loss mingled with tears of rage, but those tears were **restrained** by nobility. In Priam's eyes, godlike Achilles caught a first fleeting glimpse of himself. In a flash, he grasped Priam's superiority. Could Achilles have acted thus if a son of his had been killed? Would love for his own son have overcome his rage against his son's killer? As he gazed at Priam, Achilles' thoughts flew to his own father, far away, who, like Priam, was never to see his most beloved son again. For Achilles had chosen to follow Hector into death and glory. Achilles' rage and contempt **evaporated** into the night air, replaced by **veneration** for this most majestic of kings. He had finally met an **opponent** over whom he could not triumph. Achilles, for the first time in his life, and with great relief, submitted. He **imitated** the old king's actions, dropping to his knees and embracing Priam, tearfully promising to **obey** the king's wishes.

For a long time, Achilles wept with the king. He wept for Priam's son, for his own father, and for all sons and fathers. Above all, he wept for the needless losses our rage inflicts upon one another, and upon ourselves.

Set 2

How do living cells **generate** the energy they need? Inside living cells are specific structures called *organelles* that provide the energy necessary for life. In plants, *chloroplasts* trap sunlight and use its energy to create energy-carrying molecules. In animals, *mitochondria* create the same energy-carrying molecules, called *ATP*, by using oxygen to break down **complex** organic compounds into carbon dioxide and water. Mitochondria and chloroplasts are about the same size and have the same biochemistry as bacteria. They even have their own DNA **blueprint** and divide within the cell on their own schedule. Bacteria are known as *prokaryotic* cells because they lack most organelles. The more complex cells found in animals and plants are called *eukaryotic* cells; they contain many organelles. One of the most fascinating **hypotheses** to come out of biology in the last half century is that these key structures inside the cells of all multicellular life forms were once free-living organisms. This notion is called *endosymbiosis*.

In endosymbiosis, a "guest" and a "host" species coevolve to the point of fusion—the guest species is absorbed into a host species and spends its entire life cycle within the host. The arrangement is not parasitic. One or both of the species benefits. So, how did the precursors to eukaryotic cells acquire mitochondria- and chloroplast-like prokaryotes? In what manner could a microorganism's bodily **integrity** be breached? The evolutionary **narrative** has been reconstructed as follows: the story goes that amoeba-like precursors to eukaryotic cells assimilated all kinds of prokaryotic organisms. Most were simply broken down and absorbed, but some hardy proto-organelle organisms survived—even flourished—in the new, nutrient-rich environment.

This hypothesis can never be conclusively proven, but its plausibility has been increasingly **documented** as various lines of evidence and **observation** have converged. If true, the endosymbiotic origin of mitochondria and chloroplasts **supplants**, or at least challenges, two long-held tenets. First, we are used to seeing bacterial invasions as just that—causes of disease that constrict life functions. These ancient and **venerable** guest species have actually radically **expanded** their hosts' evolutionary horizons. Ironically, we owe our very existence to endosymbiosis. Aside from **stimulating** the development of ever more complex organisms, endosymbiosis solved a critical issue for life on Earth—the increase in oxygen levels. Early life was entirely anaerobic, meaning energy was created without oxygen. In fact, oxygen was the by-product. Oxygen, **perplexing** as it may seem, is actually a poison. This highly reactive element effectively **prohibited** the emergence of terrestrial life. But oxygen-eating proto-mitochondria filled the niche, creating an alternative energy source for their new hosts. Thus, the inclusion of these guest species into the architecture of the eukaryotic cell made complex terrestrial life possible.

Second, since all plants and animals feature these once free-living organelles, the **universality** of endosymbiosis challenges our notion of what we take to be an individual organism. The boundaries between self and environment and between individual and colony can seem **illusory** when one takes the long view of endosymbiosis. Inside our trillions of cells, we carry opportunistic little creatures whose energetic surplus fuels all the varied activities of plants and animals, from the creation of the wood pulp from which the book you're holding was manufactured to the operation of the brain that is now puzzling over this vocabulary-building exercise. So take a deep breath, and reward your oxygen-hungry mitochondria with a well-deserved treat!

Set 3

That all buildings embody the belief systems of the cultures that built them is beyond **debate**. However, not all buildings are equal. Some are **determined** more by functions common to all societies rather than by those culturally specific functions that are central to an entire belief system. For example, modern-day takeout restaurants in New York City look remarkably similar to Roman takeout restaurants still preserved at Pompeii—an L-shaped bar featuring holes for hot pots. Classic architectural monuments stand out because they provide an impressively **comprehensive** and immensely complex structural manifestation of the function that reflects, or even **defines**, a culture. Size and scale also help to denote a classic building: if you want to look closely at what a culture's priorities were, **scrutinize** the structure that required the highest investment of ingenuity, resources, and political power. The heart of a culture lies in its greatest buildings.

One such building is the Hagia (pronounced *Hi-ya*) Sophia, the Great Church of the Holy Wisdom, in Istanbul. Istanbul was once known as Constantinople—the City of Constantine, built as a new capital by the Roman emperor who had made Christianity the state religion in the fourth century A.D. Two centuries later, the western Roman empire had fallen, but the eastern empire—known to historians as the Byzantine Empire—had not merely **endured**, but was in the process of temporarily reconquering the western lands that were once Roman. Justinian, who reigned from 527 to 565, was the **architect** of this territorial expansion, which was seen by **contemporaries** as restoring the glory and power of the Roman Empire. The restoration was not merely military; Justinian also ordered the codification and clarification of all Roman law as a new, rational basis for civil order. The "Justinian Code" served as the foundation for modern-day law in most European countries.

The restoration of the glory that was Rome can also be seen in Justinian's signature building, the Hagia Sophia. After a riot that destroyed the original Hagia Sophia, and which nearly **supplanted** him, Justinian marshaled a tremendous effort to adapt secular Roman architecture to a new kind of building that epitomized Byzantine power. Unlike most pagan temples, which served mostly as a holy backdrop for outdoor ritual, the Hagia Sophia fused a unique Roman temple—the Pantheon, or "Temple of All the Gods"—with a typical secular building, the basilica, a long, rectangular hall used for law courts or markets. The Pantheon, built by the emperor Hadrian in the early second century A.D., featured a huge dome resting on a cylindrical drum. At the apex of the dome was a large hole, the oculus, which provided the only natural light. The **progress** of the disc of light from the oculus across the floor and walls of the building served to animate this architectural representation of the ordered Roman universe.

Hagia Sophia's dome rested not on a drum, but, radically, on a perfect square. To get from square walls to a circular dome, the Byzantines invented *pendentives*, curving, concave triangular forms that rise from the corners of the cube and spread toward each other, allowing for the transition from cube to hemisphere by rounding off the corners of the cube. The sides of the cube rise toward the base of the dome, progressively rounded off by the **expanding** pendentives rising from the corners until the gravestone-like curved apex touches the base of the dome. The base of the dome itself—where the four pendentives finally intersect—is punctuated by a series of windows. Hagia Sophia's dome seems to float above the building, "as though suspended from Heaven by a golden chain," as one contemporary observer put it. Arrayed around that dome-on-a-cube was a larger complex of vaulted aisles, half-domes, and upper galleries, all of which opened upward, complementing the immense central space under the dome.

Why did Justinian's architects risk putting a dome on a perfect square? No one had ever attempted this—and despite Justinian's announcement that he had surpassed Solomon as a builder, the dome fell not once but three times in the subsequent 1,500 years, first collapsing a mere thirty years after completion. The answer lies in the near-**universal** use of large religious buildings to identify imperial power structures with the Divine. Byzantine religious practice, and the central relation between that practice and Byzantine state power, **demanded** that a Roman dome be placed on a Roman basilica. The patriarch (the leader of the Byzantine church) and the emperor were seen as the two halves of the earthly manifestation of God himself, united in leading an ordered, divinely sanctioned society. Byzantine Christianity purposely cultivated the "Great Mystery" of faith, to which only the Patriarch and the Emperor were privy. All faith was mediated through these two figures via an elaborate set of rituals, just as all political power was mediated through a Byzantine court bureaucracy so complicated and convoluted that *Byzantine* entered our language as an adjective meaning "of labyrinthine **complexity**."

Citizens crowded into the Hagia Sophia to view elaborate, half-hidden rituals. Only the emperor, the patriarch, and their attendants could walk beneath the dome in the central open space. All others were packed into the aisles and galleries on the periphery with purposely half-obscured views of the proceedings. That is why Byzantine churches adopted the rectangular basilica—they appropriated the Roman form that was designed to accommodate the multitudes. Not only were the rituals semi-hidden, but full appreciation of the domed interior space of the Hagia Sophia was denied to anyone viewing it from the periphery—which meant everyone but the uppermost elite of the political system. Since that interior space was itself meant to be an architectural representation of Creation, full appreciation of Hagia Sophia's interior space meant full apprehension of Creation itself, a privilege granted only to the elite, and on which the legitimacy of its power rested. Like the Pantheon, the Hagia Sophia was designed to show that the divinely ordered universe was reflected by and embodied in the political structure of society. The implication was purposeful—the political structure was thus sanctioned by Heaven itself. **Obedience** to the regime was the **measure** not only of one's loyalty but also of one's piety. Any and all **opposition** to the regime was thus evil.

Set 4

Many students either **condemn** the SAT, refusing to have anything to do with such a misguided—even evil—test, or **disregard** it, assuming that by refusing to pay attention, the nasty test will just go away. I believe that fear causes these two reactions.

In order to test this proposition—or, in other words, to **investigate** this **hypothesis**—we need to thoroughly **analyze** a current misunderstanding of tests like the SAT. While it is true that the SAT stemmed from the intelligence-testing wing of applied psychology eighty years ago, it is no longer accurate to characterize the SAT as a **contemporary** and anachronistic manifestation of controversial IQ testing. The one clear trend in SAT history is a continual, **progressive** retreat from "puzzle-solving" item types in all tested areas. However, decades of welcome **correctives** to the SAT's IQ-testing background have yet to **persuade** many, if not most, of the public. Furthermore, many of those who **defend** the SAT in the media seem to agree with the test's detractors, holding to the **illusion** that the test measures "intelligence," whatever *that* may be. Thus, students are forced to confront a **distorted** image of the SAT in which a test designed to **plot** the achievement of acquired skills and knowledge becomes a nefarious **plot** to **exclude** the unintelligent from the rewards due to the **elect**.

WORD-PART EXERCISES

The word parts used in these exercises are from the lists of roots, suffixes, and prefixes that you have made into flashcards and studied. If you haven't done this yet, please stop and do so now. Save these exercises for reinforcement, which is their best use. Answers to these exercises can be found on page 72.

MATCHING

Match each word part with its definition. In some sets there are more word parts than definitions; in others, there are more definitions than word parts.

Set 1: Roots

___ 1. agon	A. life; living
___ 2. cog	B. to breathe; breath; spirit
___ 3. fid	C. idea; philosophy
___ 4. idio	D. cross; significant
___ 5. spir	E. personal; private
___ 6. cruc	F. society; group
___ 7. andro	G. right; law
___ 8. greg	H. struggle; content
___ 9. jur	I. to think
___ 10. viv	J. male
	K. faith; trust

Set 2: Roots

___ 1. vol	A. love; fondness for
___ 2. temp	B. to look; to see
___ 3. spec	C. bad

___ 4. sequ
___ 5. kine
___ 6. mal
___ 7. locut
___ 8. phil
___ 9. rupt
___ 10. patri
___ 11. opt

D. movement; energy
E. to speak; speech
F. to break; to sever
G. father
H. will; desire; wish
I. eye; vision
J. time; balance

Set 3: Roots

___ 1. for
___ 2. flux
___ 3. graph
___ 4. mis
___ 5. par
___ 6. phobo
___ 7. rati
___ 8. reg
___ 9. scrib
___ 10. anim
___ 11. arch

A. a written record; to write
B. equal
C. fear
D. to think; calculate
E. first; ancient; rule
F. to write; something written
G. strong
H. mind; feeling; life
I. to flow
J. hate

Set 4: Roots

___ 1. aco(u)
___ 2. chrom
___ 3. dict
___ 4. gest
___ 5. hier
___ 6. ject
___ 7. luc
___ 8. mort
___ 9. path
___ 10. tens

A. holy; sacred
B. to say; speech; word
C. light; to shine
D. to throw
E. to eat; to swallow
F. to stretch
G. to hear; hearing
H. death
I. color
J. emotion; suffering
K. to carry; to produce

Set 5: Prefixes and Suffixes

___ 1. ad
___ 2. ante
___ 3. circum
___ 4. contra

A. around
B. before; prior; in front of
C. to; toward
D. separation

___ 5.	dis	E.	over, above; around
___ 6.	epi	F.	after; along with; transfer; changed
___ 7.	meta	G.	more; beyond normal; excessive
___ 8.	peri	H.	beyond; across; through
___ 9.	hyper	I.	downward; against; contrary to
___ 10.	hypo	J.	around; near; beside
___ 11.	trans	K.	against
___ 12.	cata		

Set 6: Prefixes and Suffixes

___ 1.	a	A.	in; into; within
___ 2.	ambi	B.	bad; difficult
___ 3.	com	C.	with; together
___ 4.	dys	D.	beside; near; faulty
___ 5.	ent	E.	before; in front of
___ 6.	op	F.	both; around
___ 7.	per	G.	back; backward
___ 8.	pre	H.	toward; against; face-to-face
___ 9.	re	I.	not; without
___ 10.	sym	J.	united; together with; same
		K.	through; thoroughly

Set 7: Prefixes and Suffixes

___ 1.	ab	A.	outside of; external; away from
___ 2.	de	B.	worse; badly
___ 3.	ecto	C.	down from; reverse; remove; derived from; out of
___ 4.	eu	D.	earlier; before; forward
___ 5.	em	E.	beyond; across; through
___ 6.	im	F.	away; from; separated
___ 7.	ment	G.	result; means of or product of an action
___ 8.	mis	H.	beside; near; faulty
___ 9.	para	I.	well; good
___ 10.	pro	J.	in; on; amongst; within
___ 11.	tra		

DECIPHERING DEFINITIONS

These are words you haven't seen in this book. They are all real words containing the word parts you've been studying.

- First, categorize the words as either "positive," "negative," or "neutral" by marking each blank.
- Second, define each one in the space below (or on a separate sheet of paper) based solely on your knowledge of word parts.
- Third, look these words up in your dictionary to see how close you were.

Set 1

__ 1. circumnavigate

__ 2. patricide

__ 3. dystopia

__ 4. primal

__ 5. nominal

__ 6. expulsion

__ 7. amity

animosity

__ 8. inauguration

__ 9. interregnum

__ 10. brachiation

__ 11. infraction

__ 12. misanthropic

__ 13. ingrate

__ 14. capitation

__ 15. malediction

__ 16. metonymy

__ 17. transpiration

__ 18. archetype

__ 19. heliotropic

__ 20. diachronic

Set 2

__ 1. ambulatory

__ 2. amphitheater

___ 3. anthropogenesis

___ 4. aqueduct

___ 5. archaism

___ 6. synchronic

___ 7. microcosm

___ 8. incorporate

___ 9. gradient

___ 10. ideography

___ 11. malodorous

___ 12. circumspect

___ 13. extemporaneous

___ 14. tractable

___ 15. convivial

RELATED ROOTS

Many roots have similar meanings. List the relevant roots underneath each general meaning.

For example:

Love/Good Feeling

am; amat
grat
phil; philia

You can use the following groupings to organize your word-part flash-cards for further study.

1. To hear/to listen/sound

2. To write/writing/written record

3. Speech/to speak/to say

4. Equal/equality/equivalent

5. To look/to see/looking/sight

6. Thought/belief/mind/thinking/teaching

7. Write down three more groupings you can use to categorize your root flashcards.

   A.

   B.

   C.

RELATED PREFIXES AND SUFFIXES

Many prefixes and suffixes have similar meanings. List the relevant prefixes and suffixes underneath each general meaning.

For example:

Around

ambi; amphi
circum
epi
peri

You can use the following groupings to organize your word-part flashcards for further study.

1. Before/earlier

2. Away from/separated from

3. Not/against/downward/negatives

4. Through

5. Write down two more groupings you can use to categorize your root flashcards.

   A.

   B.

ANSWERS TO WORD-PART EXERCISES

Matching

Set 1: Roots

1. H
2. I
3. K
4. E
5. B
6. D
7. J
8. F
9. G
10. A

Set 2: Roots

1. H
2. J
3. B
4. [none]
5. D
6. C
7. E
8. A
9. F
10. G
11. I

Set 3: Roots

1. G
2. I
3. A
4. J
5. B
6. C
7. D
8. [none]
9. F
10. H
11. E

Set 4: Roots

1. G
2. I
3. B
4. K
5. A
6. D
7. C
8. H
9. J
10. F

Set 5: Prefixes and Suffixes

1. C
2. B
3. A
4. K
5. D
6. E
7. F
8. J
9. G
10. [none]
11. H
12. I

Set 6: Prefixes and Suffixes

1. I
2. F
3. C
4. B
5. A
6. H
7. K
8. E
9. G
10. J

Set 7: Prefixes and Suffixes

1. F
2. C
3. A
4. I
5. J
6. [none]
7. G
8. B
9. H
10. D
11. E

Deciphering definitions

We note below whether a word is positive, negative, or neutral by using +, –, and N, respectively. We also highlight the word part or parts. The definition we leave to you to find in your dictionary. Remember to make a word flashcard for each word.

Set 1

N	1. **circum**navigate
–	2. **patri cide**
–	3. **dys top** ia
N	4. **prim**al
N	5. **nom**inal
–	6. **ex puls** ion
+	7. **ami**ty
N	8. **in aug** uration
N	9. **inter reg**num
N	10. **brachi**ation

–	11. **in fract** ion
–	12. **mis anthro** pic
–	13. **in grat**e
N	14. **capit**ation
–	15. **male**dic**tio**n
N	16. **meto nym**y *(Hint: word parts sometimes change their spelling in different words.)*
N	17. **trans [s]pir** ation
+	18. **arch**etype
N	19. **helio trop**ic *(Hint:* helio *means "pertaining to the sun.")*
N	20. dia**chron**ic

Set 2

N	1. **ambul** atory
N	2. **amphi** theater
N	3. **anthro** po **gen** esis
N	4. **aque** duct
–	5. **arch** aism
N	6. **syn chron** ic
N	7. **micro cosm**
N	8. **in corp** orate
N	9. **grad** ient
N	10. **ideo graph** y
–	11. **mal** odorous
+	12. **circum spect**
N	13. **ex temp** oraneous
–	14. **tract** able
+	15. **con viv** ial

Related Roots

1. To hear/to listen/sound

   aco(u)
   aud
   plaud; plaus; plod; plos

2. To write/writing/written record

   scrib; script; scribe
   gram; graph

3. Speech/to speak/to say

   dic; dict; diction
   locut; loqu; loquy
   log; logue; logy; lexico
   voc; vok; vow

4. Equal/equality/equivalent

   equ; iqu
   iso
   par; pare

5. To look/to see/looking/sight

   opt; optic
   spec; spic; spect

6. Thought/belief/mind/thinking/teaching

   anim
   cog; cogit
   cred; creed; creant
   doc; doct; dog; dox
   fid; fidel
   ideo
   rati; reas
   soph; sophy

7. There are many possibilities. Here are three suggestions.

   A. Feeling; feelings; emotion(s)
   B. Strength/weakness
   C. To bring together/to break apart

Related Prefixes and Suffixes

1. Before/earlier

   ante; anter
   pre
   pro

2. Away from/separated from

   ab; abs
   apo; ap
   dis; di; dif
   ec; ecto; ex
   se

3. Not/against/downward/negatives

   a; an
   cata; cat; cath
   contra
   de
   dys
   in; im
   mis
   ob; op; of
   un

4. Through

   per
   trans; tra

5. *There are many possibilities. Here are two suggestions.*

   A. "With/within/together"
   B. "Near/beside"

FLOCABULARY

Flocabulary taps into one of the most ancient and effective learning techniques: using rhymes to memorize words and lines. Poetry itself was founded on the principle that audiences and poets would better remember poems if the lines rhymed with one another. Patterns and rhymes are easy to memorize, which is why mnemonics often use them.

Each rap in *Flocabulary* is really just a string of mnemonic devices set over catchy, popular music. The power of rhyme speaks for itself. Without rhyming, students struggle to memorize words in a vacuum, drilling themselves repeatedly without context. Take the word *mutability*, which means "the ability to change." How do you remember the definition of mutability? Enter *Flocabulary*:

Mutability is the property
that allows an entity
to change just what its gonna be

We've created two flocabulary raps using some SAT vocab. The lyrics are printed following this page. You can download the raps off our website at **www.sparknotes.com/newsat/flocabulary**. Listen to these raps in conjunction with preparing and studying your flashcards. The combination of study methods will help you learn the definitions faster.

LYRICS

FLOCABULARY

(A. Rappaport, Escher)

Can you feel it D? I can feel it.
Can you feel it E? I can feel it.
Flocabulary, can you feel it?
Flocabulary we can feel it.

[D]
I'm trying to live **vividly**, trying to stay intense,
I keep it **stoic** and **serene**, 'cause I'm calm under stress,
What's next? The sounds of my breath make rhymes seem sleeker,
A lyricist, an **elocutionist**, a public speaker,
We going long distance, rocking **fortitude** and strength,
Don't know the **destination**, but I know we go the length,
Dodging **obstacles** in our path, jumping over hurdles,
Linear and straightforward, never running in circles,
We **evade** those who chase us, they're motionless like **stasis**,
Their **semblance**, their **visages**, and their faces
Betray their **trepidation** and betray their **dismay**,
They fear and they worry because they don't know the way,

[E]
We know the way,
We're trailblazing, doing it first, **initiating**,
Like bobsledders who are Jamaican,
We're **catalysts** for your **enlightenment**, and your **illumination**,
the rebirth, the **renaissance**, we're **generating**,
We **amplify**, aliens can hear our rhymes in the sky,
we **alienate** those who don't like the volume too high,
We are a little **eccentric**, a little outside the norm,

So in a crowd of the same people, you can **discern** our form,
Make it out, like teenagers in home basements,
Lying next to each other, they are **adjacent**,
I add beauty to my rhymes so I **embellish**,
I relish my hot dog when I add relish,

[E & D]
Now everybody act like an **oscillating** fan,
And wave back and forth with your lighter in your hand,
Now **manual** could be where you look for instruction,
We flip through magazines for tips on seduction,
But manual comes from the French word for hands,
So every woman and man must clap their mains!

C'mon clap, c'mon y'all clap your mains!
Can you feel it D? I can feel it.
Can you feel it E? I can feel it.
Flocabulary, can you feel it?
Flocabulary we can feel it.

[D]
I'm the hero of this song, the **protagonist**,
Spitting lyrics like graffiti so I'm tagging this,
The **apex**, the **pinnacle**, also the **zenith**,
We're at the top of the charts, and the world is beneath us,
We're talking about expanding, but I have no attention,
I'm **digressing**, could you please repeat the question,
I **preserve** the flavor of the jam in a bottle,
I preserve my wealth cause I never play lotto,
Hip-hop is **universal**, pervading galaxies,
Plus the whole world can listen and relate back to me,
Never **neglect** the air you're breathing,
Pay attention to the sun and the season,
'cause son there's a reason,
I'm both **concave** and **convex** like crescents,
We're the state of being quiet, like **quiescence**,
Full of talents, I'm never **tacit** 'cause I hate silence,
I don't tip off the rope, I stay balanced,

Not back and forth, not forth and back,
If I'm **famished**, I better find me a snack,
If my throat's **parched**, I need something to wet it,
Lubricate my tongue so I can spit full credit,
For all the **critics** in the house, who offer **criticism**,
Who judge the beat, the flow and my lyricism,
You can **analyze** me, examine me critically,
But try to **compete** with me? That won't be easy,
If you **antagonize** me you provoke hostility in me,
Enmity, mutual, deep-seated hatred,
It's the kind of thing that must be abated,
lessened or avoided, what we got to **abstain** from,
Pop goes the weasel or the tarts in your toaster,
Up and down like **vicisssitudes** or a roller coaster,
I think we're supposed to reach a **consensus**, an agreement
But what I call concrete, you call the cement.

C'mon clap y'all c'mon clap your mains!
Can you feel it D? I can feel it.
Can you feel it E? I can feel it.
Flocabulary, can you feel it?
Flocabulary we can feel it.

QUANTIFY

(A. Rappaport, H.H. Blake)

When I was **nascent**, being formed in my mama's belly,
It was so cozy I wanted to stay there forever, **indefinitely**,
It was all **obscure**, totally **caliginous** and dark,
I could hear the **melodious** sound of my mama's beating heart, then BOOM
I was born shrunken like a prune, a former plum,
Shot out the womb like a gun into the room and soon
Started crying, bawling, **vocalizing**, weeping,
My **behavior belied** the fact I wanted to be speaking,
Gave it away, gave my cord to the doctor carving,
I looked more **singular** and strange than E.T. or Marvin the Martian,
Outlandish, my eyes were **resplendent** full of many different colors,

Brilliant like mother's, my genetic **blueprint** like my brothers,
So we resemble each other, like **replicas**, **models**, or clones,
My mama took me home, called my grandma on the phone,
To tell her of the **melodrama**: I'd been born,
Just to tell her the **momentous** news: I had been born.

I said you could count on me,
But you can't quantify the qualities of my life

When I was ten I tried to rap in front of my school,
It was a **debacle**, a failure, I felt like a fool,
I'll give you **testimony**, I will tell you the truth
It was a **fiasco**, a **catastrophe**, and here is the proof,
I tried to rhyme the word "rap" with "wrap" imagine that,
Those **homonyms** will give you a sense of where I was at,
I used to be a **neophyte**, a beginner, I didn't know how to write,
A **novice**, so I had to study all night,
I did **assiduous** work, paid constant attention,
I studied the rappers **diligently**, don't have to mention,
How I **venerate** the **venerable** creators of this music,
I honor those who invented it so we could bounce to it,
When I **admire** them, I love them, I give them **adulation**,
Can you say you love hip-hop with no **hesitation**,
No waiting like a waiter at the side of your table,
In the **periphery** of your sight, angled like right.

I said you could count on me,
But you can't quantify the qualities of my life

Now I'm writing a **novel** novel,
"A novel novel I don't get it,"
A novel that's new, I wrote this old novel but no one read it,
So I shredded it, it made my readers sleepy like a **sedative**,
I come from my mother, so I guess I'm her **derivative**,
I might be **beguiling** or tricking you, to say that at the age of twenty-two,
A blood clot stopped the blood from flowing through my veins,
I let it **coagulate**, this plot thickens, just like a stew,
But I survived, emerged **robust** and **hardy** like them boys,
I talk in a **vociferous** voice, make a lot of noise

It was **inane**, I was born with rapping in these veins but pardon,
I've got to **nurture** and **cultivate** it like a garden,
I wasn't **engendered** yesterday, but I feel like I'm just starting,
I like to **ruminate** on life, sit back and contemplate it, how I made it,
I traded my soul for this vocal box, never studied geology, but, I know what rocks,
This is the **sanctified** marriage of Test Prep and Hip-Hop

I said you could count on me,
But you can't quantify the qualities of my life

ABOUT THE AUTHOR

Doug Tarnopol brings a unique mix of talents and experience to SparkNotes and the New SAT *Power Tactics* series. He has taught and tutored students of all backgrounds and advised both students and parents on preparing for the SAT. Doug graduated magna cum laude from Cornell University in 1992, earning a B.A. in History. He continued his work in the history and sociology of science at the University of Pennsylvania, receiving an M.A. in 1996.

While in graduate school, Doug began teaching SAT test-prep classes. After completing his graduate work, Doug moved to New York City and continued working in test prep, adding PSAT, SCI HI, SAT II: Writing, SAT II: Math, GMAT, and other courses to his repertoire. In 1999, Doug became a curriculum developer, designing instructional material for state proficiency exams.

Doug also writes fiction and poetry. He is an avid drummer, biker, and reader. He currently lives in Metuchen, New Jersey.

SPARKNOTES
Power Tactics for the New SAT

The Critical Reading Section

Reading Passages

Sentence Completions

The Math Section

Algebra

Data Analysis, Statistics & Probability

Geometry

Numbers & Operations

The Writing Section

The Essay

Multiple-Choice Questions: Identifying Sentence Errors, Improving Sentences, Improving Paragraphs

The New SAT

Test-Taking Strategies

Vocabulary Builder